Basic Concept of Obligation

In the wake of final crusades

AR Sheikh

Contents

Basic Concept of Religious Obligations

God draws towards him anyone He wants to, and guides the one in the right direction who seeks His guidance.

There are two motives of human actions. The first one is the intent. The saying regarding this is:

> "The reward of actions depends upon the intention".

The second motive of human actions is knowledge and understanding of the obligations, in this context religious.

The first source for understanding Islam is Quran and for further insight there is Hadith or in other words Sunnah of the Holy Prophet PBUH. Sunnah includes the actions as well as saying of the Prophet PBUH.

Religious Duties and their Pre-requisites

In this context, three things are very basic:

- First, we should act on these.
- Second, we should propagate these.

- Third, we should establish these Islamic regulations.

First Duty

Acting on Islam

Four terms are to be explained:

- Islam
- Obedience
- Abstinence
- Supplication

Islam

This first term refers to the fact that one should submit his will to God. Using the basic terminologies, the clause would be to surrender or the give up resistance

Quran Says!

"O you who believe, enter Islam completely".

It implies either take it all or leave it all. There is no such concept as partial obedience or partial transgression. Because, partial obedience would be counted as no obedience.

Obedience

This term furthers the insight fullness on Islam. The obedience with sincerity and hearty intent is required, Quran says!

"And, obey God, and his prophet (PBUH) and if you ignore them then know that prophet's responsibility is to give the message of God to the people and not more than that".

So, thinking that if one obeys God partially, that would suffice, is a very wrong notion, rather a misconception, The least would be to at least struggle to achieve the level of total obedience.

Abstinence

This is the third important term and it means fearing God and so refraining from the unlawful. Or, not breaching God's laws because of the fear of punishment. God says in Quran!

'O you who believe, refrain from the unlawful, as it is required, and beware that death must not reach you in the state of infidelity'.

Worship

This is the fourth important term. It implies that one should devote himself to the cause of pleasing God. Quran say!

'I (Allah) have created Jins and human beings to worship me'.

Partial Obedience Will be Unacceptable

In this regard, Quran states,

- o 'Do you accept one part of our book and deny the other? Any one and among you who does that would be punished gravely in the hereafter and will be disgraced in the life of this world. And , God is not unaware of what you do!'

- o 'Hypocrites will be in deepest pits of Hell and will not find anyone to help them'.

- o 'O believers! Why do you preach what you yourself do not do? This displeases God to a great extent'.

Fulfilling the Islamic Obligations

A great Islamic philosopher Dr Mohammad Iqbal has implied in his poetry that the very thought of religious obligations shivers him.

A companions of the Prophet (PBUH) narrates, " the Prophet said, five things that there is only one God, and that Mohammad PBUH is his last Prophet, praying regularly, giving in charity/alms, performing pilgrimage of the house of Allah 'Kaba' and fasting in the month of Ramzan.

One must keep in mind that these five pillars of Islam are very fundamental and fulfil its requirements as a religion. But, as a complete system, it demands more. If one tries to sketch it out like Dr. Israr Ahmad has , the first pillar is more like a foundational base and the other four are the supporting structures of the building, i.e. testifying lie in the foundation, prayers, fasting, alms/charity and pilgrimage are the four structural supports. It is obvious that this building cannot be erected without these said pillars. However, these five elements will complete the first level only. On top of this floor will lay the structure or building of Islam as a complete system.

Second Duty

Passing message of Islam to the others especially the ones who don't know it or about it.

In this context four terms are important.

Preaching

For spreading Islam, it is important to propagate the teachings of it to people, especially the ones other then the Muslim communities.

Quran says!

'O Prophet (PBUH), pass on the message that has been given to you by God'.

Inviting

It implies inviting people toward God and the final religion. God says!

'And whose speech would be better than that of a person who invites towards God'.

'Invite people , to the path of the God, with wisdom, and argue nicely with the ones who resist'.

Instructing good and forbidding bad

A Hadith Says!

Anyone who sees an unlawful act should stop it if he has the power. If not that, that person should stop it by saying a few words. If even not that, then that person should at least think of that bad act as a bad act, and this is the last level of faith.

Another narration says!

'And after that there will not be a hint of faith left'.

Declaring on People

This is the fourth term in this context and it implies that for the record one should take the testimony of people that they have received the message. The point is to declare that the responsibility of passing the message on has been fulfilled and if and surely on the day of resurrection believers will be asked, then, this testimony of people will suffice, which implies that one can reply saying, "God! I have pass your message on".

Quran Says!

"And what will it be like on the day when we will raise a person to testify for each nation, and O messenger, we will make you a witness on them".

On another place, the holy book says!

"And we have made you a nation in the middle, so that you become witness on mankind, and messenger PBUH, become witness on you".

On the final pilgrimage address, the Holy Prophet PBUH had made it a point imperatively that the ones who are present now should take the message to the ones who are not here.

Third Obligation

To Establish Religion

Quran has clearly stated.

"Religion in the sight of the God is Islam".

We often state that Islam is a complete system of life, yet we do not fulfil the right of this claim. This is to be kept in mind that until and unless the regulations of Islam are established as a functioning system, the thought would be considered as utopia because the practical application is not there.

Raising the name of God

It implies that one should raise the status of God, Quran in this regard says, 'And raise the status of God'!

On another place, it says , 'no doubt, the order is that of God alone'.

This implies that there must be such a system where in the absolute sovereignty belongs to God. It is important to mention and that Islamic philosopher of subcontinent revived this concept.

Quran reminds!

"O People, know this well, the life of this world is temporary like a small play, the real life is that of hereafter may people understand".

"And do these people not understand that they will resurrect one day? All human kind will stand before God and be held accountable for their actions".

The whole point of this struggle is raising the status of God. The practiced example of such a system was the one established by the Holy Prophet PBUH in the State of Madina and in that system the supreme authority was that of God, the one and only absolute sovereign.

Establishing Religion as a System

With regard to this responsibility this is the second term. Quran has stated, "Establish the religion, and do not part in to groups in this matter".

'O messenger, clearly say to the people of the book, that you are not on the standard set by God Unless you establish the old and new testament of your Bible which was revealed to you by God'.

This is a wakeup call for the Muslims. If we do not establish Islam, then surely, we are not on the standard set by God, which implies, politico-socio-economical system of global social justice and not just the rituals of daily routine.

Religion ought to be for God

Quran states!

"And fight the pagans, to the point where there is no evil remaining and religion becomes that for God".

On another place!

"O believers, battle them until the evil perishes and religion because all that of God".

Some modernists say that religion can only be practiced on personal level and it cannot be applied to political or social matters. They quote the example of British ruling the India subcontinent without forcing practice of faith on personal level. Their slogan is referral to keeping religion as personal law only. This way of thinking is highly corrupted. In the modern time, there has to be a way or a set of ways to incorporate religious bindings in the political, social and economic matters of a state. Presidential or parliamentary system can be moulded via legislation and incorporation of Islamic principles and should be.

Dominance of the Right Religion

"And it is God who has sent the messenger PBUH, with the true belief system so that it dominates all other forms of faith".

Religion has evolved from the beginning of human civilization. Before the final form of the religion which happens to be Islam, the religions were local not global in extent. No previous religion could be established in its true form but Islam in the state of Madina, because of resistance over- whelming the movement. On the other hand, the non faith systems made by man at different stages of history have completely or partially failed either in clashes or themselves over time. So, now, it is high time for human kind to realize the importance of Islam as the final form of the religion and that as a complete system of life. It is noteworthy that civilization have clashed and now religions will clash at a global level. The whole point of re-appearance of Jesus Christ PBUH is the establishment of the global system of social justice, 'Islam'.

It clearly implies that alongside obeying the instructions of God, passing on his message to the masses is the primary obligation of the believers. Quran was revealed in Arabic but after the prophet PBUH and his rightly guided caliphs, this propagation was compromised by the so-termed Muslims rulers especially the ones in Ottoman Empire and then the Arabs because they compromised Caliphate and later indulged in the worldly leisure and entertainment. Now the responsibility lies mainly on the non Arab Muslims as the Poet of the East has pointed out!

"Where the leader of the Arab felt the cool breeze coming

That is my land, that is my land"

This refers to the Indian subcontinent especially considering the revivalist contributions of scholars during the second millennium of Islam from here. It is of interest to revise that sketch which put faith in foundation. Prayers, fasting, alms and pilgrimage in the basement as four pillars, the instructing of good and forbidding from bad as the first floor as well as declaring on people. And the second and the top floor is the establishing of religion of Islam as a system and its dominance over the other systems. This is the fundamental assertion, which every Muslim has to include in his duties as a mission plan.

The three requirements of the obligations of Islam

The first requirement is Jihad and it has three types

The first type of Jihad is self control.

Answering the question of his companion, the Prophet PBUH replied, the best form of Jihad is self control which is submitting ones will to God.

Another narration of the Prophet PBUH is!

"Fight your wishes as you fight your enemies".

Jihad with Quran

Quran states!

"O Prophet PBUH struggle against the enemies of Islam with Quran", which is Jihad in its refined form.

Enemies of Islam were infidels and pagans of the time of Prophet Mohammad PBUH.

The elaboration would be, learning faith and practice of religion from Quran.

Passing it on the others, and when needed, arguing with people with the ethics of polite discussion as well as reasoning. In this context, the ways of prophet PBUH will be regard as the perfect example.

Fighting in the way of God

It is worth noting that there are no privilege classes in Islam. Rich, poor, authoritative, weak, strong and all the levels and communities are to be treated justly with equity. The initial stage of the movement in the society would be that of passive resistance because initially the believers are few and resistance is stronger and the strategy has to be that of survival. Once the group expands so does its strength, that would be the stage of active resistance which can be in the form of organizations and movements until and unless the situation demands self defence, the use of force or any kind of arms will be strictly forbidden.

The sole purpose is peaceful resistance to the wrong systems or wrong unjust components of systems functioning in the society. The last phase is active resistance in terms of armed conflict, now this is only when a state has been established or has to be established and there is a legion or army of Muslims, which fights for the rights of believers, or for their very defence. Again, the armed conflict is a state matter and so the responsibility of military of a Muslim state but first the principles have to be established within the Muslim society. Hence, the militant groups are just not allowed in any case because they only add fuel to fire and exacerbate the problems leading to civil wars. But it has to be understood and believed that without incorporating the principles of Quran and Sunnah, a Muslim army will not truly represent the force of Islam, and without Islamic principles incorporated, the army would just be a state military which does not suffice for the propagation and establishment of Islam globally. The peak of conflict so is armed engagement, 'Qital in Arabic'.

Quran States!

"And people who are being oppressed and fought against , are allowed to fight back, because God is capable of helping them".

God loves his people who fight in his way like an iron wall.

Hadith narrates!

"A person who died without intending to fight in the way of God, died a hypocrite".

Second Obligation.

Establishing a Group, 'Nonviolent and Unarmed'
Prophet PBUH said!

I give you five instructions!

    i.   Form a group

    ii.   Listen to your leader

    iii.   Obey your leader

    iv.   Migrate in the way of God.

    v.   Fight in the way of God.

Third Obligation

This is the third and crucial obligation. The members have to take an oath to listen and obey their leader, who has to be a practicing Muslim well aware and applier of the religious principles and discipline. This way the discipline of the group can be achieved. If the struggle to propagate religion requires leaving the land then it has to be done and it would be the highest of sacrifices just like fighting in the way of God is the height of the struggle in preaching and propagating Islam. Further there are many sects of Muslims so they have to pray and fast according to their denomination, but when it comes to preaching and propagation, then, they are supposed to listen to and obey the group leader not their local mosque leaders in the prayers who are not practicing or active members of the stated non-sectarian group. So Muslims from any sect can join such a group, unify for this revolutionary cause and propagate Islam in accordance with the guidelines highlighted in the cited text above. It has to be reminded here that

Dr. Mohammad Iqbal was the founding father of the revival of this concept in Indian subcontinent. Molana Abu ul Ala maududi succeeded him in the pursuit and then Dr. Israr Ahmed furthered it to a great extent.

Caliphate

Quran says !

"And Remember when your lord said to the angels! Verily I am going to appoint a vicegerent in the earth".

This clearly implies that man is only a vicegerent, and , in his own right he, does not possess sovereignty, and so, sovereignty belongs to God, and God only. The appropriate term would be absolute sovereignty, which belongs to God only.

On another place, Quran says!

"O, David! Verily we have made you a vicegerent in the earth."

Almighty has further said!

"Allah has promised those among you who believe and do righteous good deeds that he will certainly grant them Caliphate in land."

Therefore, man is a vicegerent and absolute sovereignty belongs to God only.

Implementation in Modern Times

Following points are noteworthy in this context:

System of Caliphate on the pattern Prophet hood as a term is applicable to the establishment of state of Madina by the Holy Prophet (PBUH) and also to the time of the rightly guided Caliphs, i.e. the first four caliphs of Islamic society/history after the Holy Prophet (PBUH). The Islamic caliphate will once again be established in the world according to the prophecies of the Holy Prophet (PBUH). However, the era of rightly guided caliphate will never be recreated as it was established for the first time. The substantiation of this argument would be as follows:

The age of rightly guided caliphate was an addendum or appendix of the age of the prophet hood itself and on Mohammad PBUH the institution of the prophet hood has come to an end.

The four rightly guided caliphs of Islam were trained and educated by the Holy Prophet (PBUH) himself, who had purified the souls of his companions to the utmost degree.

There was an unambiguous and clear cut hierarchy among the companions of the Holy Prophet PBUH as to who were the ten of them given the news of paradise in this life and who were the people of the first battle, "Badr" an so on.

Society at that time was tribal in character which meant that instead of having an adult franchise it was enough to take the opinions of elders of each clan.

Therefore, now, we should take the principles and ideas of the model of Prophet Mohammad (PBUH) and the rightly guided caliphs, and then in- corporate these in the political institutions, that have been developed in the civilized contemporary world as a result of the continuous process of social evolution.

As far as the details of state and government functioning is concerned, there is no binding structure provided in fact, all the various forms of government that are in practice today are permissible in Islam. From the Islamic view point, it does not make much difference if the government is federal, con- federal, unitary, and rather it is parliamentary or presidential.

But there are basic principles and solid guidelines which are as follow with regard to the government frame work:

- Sovereignty belongs to Almighty Allah alone.
- No legislation can be done at any level which is totally or partially repugnant to the teaching of Quran and Sunnah; and
- Full citizenship of the state is for Muslims only, while non-Muslims are protected minority.

Caliphate in Pakistani Perspective

The following points are note worthy.

o With the adoption of 'Objectives Resolution', on march 12,1949, in the very principle it was acknowledged that sovereignty belongs to Allah, and, the authority delegated to us by the real sovereign is to be used within the limits of Quran and Sunnah.

o In addition to the Objectives Resolution we have this imperative to limit all legislation within the very bounds set by Holy Quran and Prophet Mohammad's (PBUH) Sunnah , in article 227-1 of the constitution, which says, " all the existing laws shall be brought in conformity with the very injunctions of Islam as laid down in the Holy Quran and Sunnah, and no law shall be enacted which is repugnant to such injunctions. "

○ Establishment of 'Federal Shariat Court' was a step in the right direction. However the various restrictions placed on it, have made it somewhat ineffective with respect of Islamization of laws, whereas, the supremacy of God with respect to his laws must be absolute and without exceptions.

○ In the constitution, it must be made clear that no political party can include anything in its manifesto that is repugnant to Quran and Sunnah. The parties manifestoes could be challenge in the Federal Shariat Court and it will then decide the dispute in such a case.

- If the non-Muslims are in a big number then, separate consultative bodies for various communities of non Muslims can be formed that can advise the parliament regarding minority affairs.

- The president will be called "Khalifa Al Muslimeen" and he will be Caliph of the Muslims belonging to a particular country. Islamic state is based on collective vicegerency of the Muslims, and the Muslims will delegate this right to one man. Khalifah will be a Muslim male, not less than 40 years of age, as this is the age of maturity according to Quran, and he will have to pass a very strict and thorough screening before he is given the chair to run for this very office.

References

- Dr. Israr Ahmed, Deene Faraiz Ka Jame Tasawur.

- Dr. Israr Ahmed, Historical Overview of the Iqbal's thought.

- Dr. Israr Ahmed, A Constitutional and Legislative Framework of the Caliphate in the Modern Times.

Printed in Great Britain
by Amazon

77471076R00026